Wer lebt

Gedichte

Who Lives

Poems

Wer lebt
Gedichte

Who Lives
Poems

Elisabeth Borchers

Translated from the German by Caroline Wilcox Reul

Tavern Books

PORTLAND

Copyright © 1986 Elisabeth Borchers.
Translation Copyright © 2017 Caroline Wilcox Reul.
All rights reserved.
Printed in the United States of America.

Tavern Books receives support from the Oregon Arts Commission,
a state agency funded by the State of Oregon.

Translation of this work was supported by a grant from the Goethe-Institut, which is funded by the German Ministry of Foreign Affairs.

Cover art: Rachel Mulder, *Collection*, 2016. Typewriter ink on paper, collaged, 7.5 x 10 inches. Copyright © Rachel Mulder. Courtesy of the artist.

Borchers, Elisabeth, 1926 - 2013
Reul, Caroline Wilcox

ISBN-13: 978-1-935635-74-1 (paperback)
ISBN-13: 978-1-935635-75-8 (hardcover)

LCCN: 2017935796

First German edition published by Suhrkamp Verlag, Frankfurt, 1986.

FIRST TAVERN BOOKS EDITION

98765432 First Printing

TAVERN BOOKS
Union Station
800 NW 6th Avenue #255
Portland, Oregon 97209
www.tavernbooks.org

INHALT | CONTENTS

Notizen auf dem Lande
Notes from the Countryside

Notizen auf dem Lande	*14*
Notes from the Countryside	*15*
Von der Zeit	*22*
Of Time	*23*
Ein paar Dichter	*26*
Der Damalige	
Der Alltägliche	
Der Schweigsame	
A Few Poets	*27*
The Former One	
The Common One	
The Silent One	
Die vielen Bücher	*30*
So Many Books	*31*
Repetition in der Literatur	*32*
Repetitio in Literature	*33*

Machen wir uns einen Reim
Let's Make It Rhyme

Ein gereimtes Gedicht	*36*
A rhyming poem	*37*
Machen wir uns einen Reim	*38*
Wie schön kann er sein	
Ein Gedicht am Morgen	
Schon wieder keine Zeile	
Es lebe die Not	
Let's Make It Rhyme	*39*
How sweet it can be	
At dawn a poem	
Yes sir, another day	
May trouble thrive	

Kondolationen
Condolences

Bericht über Horst K. oder Die Besserung des Menschen	*48*
Report on Horst K., or The Rehabilitation of the Individual	*49*
Der Hirtenknabe von Lenbach	*52*
The Shepherd Boy by Lenbach	*53*
Der Augenblick	*56*
The Moment	*57*
Grablied	*58*
Funeral Song	*59*
Der Tod eines Mädchens	*60*
Death of a Girl	*61*
Stillstand	*62*
Standstill	*63*
Um Mitternacht	*64*
At Midnight	*65*

Von anderen bedenklichen Anlässen
Of Other Questionable Occasions

Möglichkeiten	*68*
Possibilities	*69*
Reden wir nicht mehr von Landschaft	*70*
Let's not talk about landscape anymore	*71*
Traum	*72*
Dream	*73*
Verweigerung der Aussage	*74*
Refusal to Testify	*75*
Utopie	*76*
Utopia	*77*
Erinnerung	*78*
Memory	*79*
Protokoll	*80*
Statement	*81*
Falsches Lied	*82*
A Different Song	*83*
An ein Kind	*84*
To a Child	*85*

Vom Öffnen des Fensters
On Opening the Window

Morgens	*88*
In the Morning	*89*
Liebes Land	*90*
Dear Country	*91*
Billionenfache Vergrößerung	*92*
Magnified by a Trillion	*93*
Pausenzeichen	*94*
Signature Tune	*95*
Bericht vom Ende der Belagerung einer Person	*96*
Report on the Liberation of a Person Under Siege	*97*

Wer lebt
Who Lives

Alter jüdischer Friedhof im Mai	*100*
Old Jewish Cemetery in May	*101*
Der Olivenbaum im Garten Gethsemane	*102*
The Olive Tree in the Garden of Gethsemane	*103*
Alte Uhr	*104*
Old Clock	*105*
Einfache Dinge	*106*
Simple Things	*107*
Beständige Dinge	*108*
Reliable Things	*109*
Erinnerung an Arp	*110*
Memory of Arp	*111*
Ordnung	*112*
Order	*113*
Das Licht gib uns heute	*114*
Give us this day the light	*115*
Wanderungen	*116*
Journeys	*117*

Herbst	*118*
Autumn	*119*
Die 7 Stationen eines langen künstlich beleuchteten Gangs	*120*
The 7 Stations of a Long Artificially Lit Passage	*121*
Trauerbänder	*122*
Als sie gegangen war	
Ich betrete nicht den Festsaal der Sätze	
Kein Wort fällt tief	
Black Bands of Mourning	*123*
When she went	
I will not enter the ballroom of sentences	
No word falls far	
Kaleidoskop	*128*
Kaleidoscope	*129*
Was alles braucht's zum Paradies	*130*
All You Need for Paradise	*131*

Notizen auf dem Lande

Notes from the Countryside

Notizen auf dem Lande

1

Lautlos decken die Dachdecker das Dach,
erfindet der Töpfer den Topf,
vor neunhundert Jahren starben
hier Kinder an Pest.
Lautlos steht es geschrieben.

2

Der Mann auf der Straße hat geseufzt.
Weil ich gerade Herrn Aghios Buch lese,
verstehe ich die Bewandtnis
und übernehme während ich weitergehe
Herrn Aghios Empfindung.

3

Der Tag dehnt sich
bis es Abend wird,
und erleichtert
sinkt er zurück.

4

Die Glocke schlägt
ruht aus
und schlägt und schlägt und schlägt.

Notes from the Countryside

1

Silently the roof tilers tile the roof,
the potters invent the pot,
nine hundred years ago
children died of plague here.
Silently it is written.

2

The man on the street let out a groan.
Because I am reading Old Aghios' book,
I understand why
and feel, as I keep walking,
how Aghios feels.

3

The day stretches out
till it's evening,
and relieved
it falls back.

4

The bell rings
pauses
and rings and rings and rings.

Sieben Jahre noch
doch nicht mehr lang
und wir reden von einander
als seien wir gestern gewesen.

5

Einen Brief schreibe ich dir,
um ganz sicher zu sein,
daß wir nicht sterben, jetzt.
Um ganz sicher zu sein,
daß wir nicht sterben,
zeige ich dir die Krone aus Messing
über dem Zifferblatt
der bleichen Uhr.

6

In der Ferne herrscht Friede.
Das sanfte Licht
trägt ihn näher heran,
bis er am Widerstand,
der wir sind,
zerbricht.

7

Ich nehme die Pose
des Denkers ein:
Wenn ich heute nicht komme,

Seven more years
it's not very long
and we'll talk about each other
as if we were yesterday.

5

I write you a letter
so I can be really sure
we won't die, now.
So I can be really sure
we won't die,
I show you the brass crown
above the dial
of the pale watch.

6

Peace reigns in the distance.
The gentle light
carries it closer and closer,
until it shatters
on the obstacle
that is us.

7

I take on the pose
of *The Thinker:*
If I don't come today,

so komme ich morgen.
Sag es dir täglich,
morgen ist bald.

8

Wenn ich X lese,
werde ich schreiben. Was er schreibt
ist erreichbar für den, der sich
täuschen läßt über das noch nicht
Geschriebene.

9

Wenn ich Y lese,
lese ich Geschichten vom Baum
der Geschichten. Und lese, wohin
ich auch schaue, die Übersetzung
des Fremdwortes
Leben.

10

Wenn ich Z lese,
buchstabiere ich das Wort
Gedächtnis und staunend stürze
ich in die mich blendende
Verarmung.

then maybe tomorrow.
Tell yourself every day
tomorrow is soon.

8

When I read X,
I will write. What he writes
is accessible for those who
fool themselves about things not yet
written.

9

When I read Y,
I read stories from the tree
of stories. And read, everywhere
I look, the translation
of the borrowed word
life.

10

When I read Z,
I spell the word
memory and fall, amazed,
into its blinding
poverty.

11
Dieser Kopf
dieses Gehäuse
für Elemente
unzuverlässiger Art
für Glück und Schmerz
so ein Gesindel

12
Vergiß.
Hinter uns
in hellen Stücken
fällt bald schon
jenseits der Länder
und schönen Gewänder
der Schnee.

11

This head,
this shell
for elements
of the unreliable kind,
for happiness and pain,
such a sorry lot.

12

Forget.
Behind us,
in bright pieces,
beyond countries
and fine cloaks,
the snow will soon
be falling.

Von der Zeit

1

Du kommst und gehst
und ich erkenne nicht
gehörst du zu mir
oder bist du vergeblich
und falsch.

2

Bist du es
wenn die Dächer aus Schiefer
deutlicher werden und stark,
es droht ein erstes Gebell.

3

Wo bist du versteckt
aus Angst vor den Schlägen,
zuerst nur ein wenig
und dann halbtot.

4

Schöne Zeit
Gold und silbernes Geschirr,
es könnte sein,
wir vergäßen zu essen.

Of Time

1

You come and go
and I can't tell
do you belong to me
or are you pointless
and false.

2

Is it you
when the slate roofs
grow sharper and strong,
when the barking threatens to begin.

3

Where are you hiding
afraid of the strikes
at first just a little,
then half to death.

4

Time so beautiful,
table set with gold and silver,
we might sit
and forget to eat.

5

Zwei Tage
möchte ich besitzen.
Den einen für das Unumgängliche.
Den zweiten
für dich.
Aber was ist das.

6

Die Tage der Commune
sind vorüber
und Rimbaud ist ein Dichter gewesen.
Vier Jahre lang.
Komm, gehn wir hinüber.

7

Doch gegenwärtig bist du,
wenn der Zug die Stadt verläßt
auf Mailand zu.
Wenn sich alles bewegt,
stehst du still
und nennst mich
dein liebstes Kind.

5

Two days
I wish I could own.
One for the unavoidable.
The second
for you.
But what is that.

6

The days of the Commune
are past,
and Rimbaud was once a poet.
For four years.
Come, let's cross over.

7

And yet you are there
when the train leaves the city
for Milan.
When everything is motion,
you stand still
and call me
your favorite child.

Ein paar Dichter

Nach der Lektüre von Gedichten
in einer literarischen Zeitschrift

Der Damalige

Er ist wieder da.
Ein Rückfall in die Begabung
von gestern
und schreibt ein Gedicht.
Ich horche
nicht mehr wie damals
als uns die Jugend zunichte machte
und groß.

Der Alltägliche

Er kennt keine Blockaden.
Auch die Rasur ist ein Thema,
das Blut leuchtet
wie Woyzeck dem Büchner.
Nur schreibend bist du ein Dichter
nur so.
Mit einem Kopf der dich trennt

A Few Poets

After reading poems
in a literary journal

The Former One

Here he is again.
Falling back into the talent
of yesterday
and he writes a poem.
I no longer listen
as I did back then
when youth undid us
and made us great.

The Common One

He knows no blocks.
Shaving is also a topic,
the blood lights up
like *Woyzeck* does for Büchner.
You are only a poet when writing
only then.
With your head separating you

von dir und den anderen
im Schwindel
der die Stufe als Abgrund erkennt
daß dich schaudert.

DER SCHWEIGSAME

Kein Wort gelingt, schreibt er,
kein Wort.
Und schreibt und schreibt.
Das Schweigen, schreibt er,
ohne Antrieb, Zeit noch Gegenwart
und schreibt
daß es die Seiten schwärzt
bis zur Unlesbarkeit.
Du schöne Kunst,
bewundernd halt ich ein.

from yourself and from others
in a spin,
recognizing with a shudder
a step is the abyss.

The Silent One

Words fail, he writes,
all of them.
And he writes and writes.
Silence, he writes,
without drive, time or presence
and he writes
blackens the pages with it
until it's unreadable.
Oh you beautiful art,
in wonder I pause.

Die vielen Bücher

und ist ein langes Wort,
sagt Danton.
Da warteten sie.

    Diese vielen Bücher, denke ich.
    Heine und Benn
    und Brecht.
    Die vielen zuvor.
    Die vielen danach.
    Verweilen, Lieben,
    Vergessen.

Und das Leben,
sagt Danton.
Da mußte er sterben.

    Ich sehe die weite Landschaft *und*
    das die Wärme
    und Kälte umfassende Haus.

So Many Books

and is a long word,
Danton says.
So they waited.

> All these books, I think.
> Heine and Benn
> and Brecht.
> So many before.
> So many after.
> To linger, love,
> to forget.

And life,
Danton says.
So he had to die.

> I see the wide open landscape *and*
> the house that holds
> the warmth and cold.

Repetition in der Literatur

Jugend zum Beispiel.
Die scharfen Empfindungen
die inszenierten Entblößungen
das überhöhte Tempo des Gefühls
die Starre
die Berechenbarkeit der Magie
Jedwede Äußerung der Sterne
der Sonne himmlisches Geblüt
das grünende Tal
und das ewig sich fortschreibende
immer zu kurz kommende Gedicht.

Repetitio in Literature

Youth, for example.
The fierce sensitivities
the staged revelations
the heady rush of emotion
the unyielding spirit
the dependability of magic
the stars' every utterance
the sun's heavenly birthright
the budding of the valley
and the poem, ever writing itself
and always falling short.

Machen wir uns einen Reim

Let's Make It Rhyme

Ein gereimtes Gedicht ist schöner als keins.
Nimm deinen Lauf.
Ich nehme die Folgen in Kauf
und ziehe die Konsequenz
bis ins Unendliche.
Das ist fern.

Oh diese Sterne.

Sie treiben mich aus meinem Plan.
Ein einziger hätte genügt
und meine Pflicht getan.

A RHYMING POEM is better than none.
So run your path
I'll accept the aftermath
and change my ways
beyond the end of time.
Now that is far.

Oh these stars.

They lure me off my course.
With just a single one
my job could have been done.

Machen wir uns einen Reim

Wie schön kann er sein
(doch ein m ist noch lange kein n).
Wie schön flatterhaft
steht er zwischen Tür und Angel.

Er kann in der Zukunft lesen
als sei sie gewesen.
Nach dem Gewicht fragt er nicht.
Wer weiß, daß er gebraucht wird
hält aus. Als Schaf oder Hirt.

Vom Zuckerbrot zum Liebestod ist nur
ein Schritt. Komm, geh doch mit.
Wird mir nicht bang bei so viel Gewalt?
Mir wird alt. Gedankenstrich
Geh. Laß mich im Stich.

Let's Make It Rhyme

How sweet it can be
(though an m is by no means a t).
Like a fickle friend
who knocks but won't step in.

It sees the future coming
as if it had passed.
It doesn't ask if you sow or reap.
You can endure when you are sure
you're needed, as a shepherd or a sheep.

From sweet talk to hemlock is
only a step away. Come on and stay.
Am I getting scared as these forces unfold?
No just old. Heavy sigh.
Go on, leave me high and dry.

Ein Gedicht am Morgen
zwei Hände voll Sorgen
wie stabil wäre das.
Das wäre, zu zweit,
ein Stück Ewigkeit.

Auch am Abend wär es mir recht.
Wer die Qual hat, hat die Wahl.
Statt dessen geschieht
ein Mord.
Dort, schau doch hin.
Und schon erfüllen mich
Ruhe und Eintracht
zur Nacht.

At dawn a poem
a handful of woe
how balanced does that seem.
Together they would be
a little piece of eternity.

A poem at dusk would also do.
If you're spoiled, you'll have to choose.
And something gets
the ax.
Well look at this.
It's already night,
peace and harmony
envelop me tight.

Schon wieder keine Zeile geschrieben,
mein Herr. Schon wieder dieses Geplärr
wer ist erkoren
wer gibt sich verloren?
Das Leben mißt sich
an Produktivität.
Zu spät. Spricht der Herr.
Wer erntet, der sät.
Und der Knecht, wie überall
siehe, er geht auch hier in den Stall.

Yes sir, another day staring at a
blank page. Yet another bout of rage
who will they choose
which of us will lose?
Crank it out
to get ahead.
Deadline's passed, the Man said.
He who reaps, sows again.
And the hack, as everywhere
you will find, goes back to the grind.

Es lebe die Not. Wer sie hat
ist noch lange nicht tot.

Zünd das Licht an im Verstand.
Nur so überlebst du
vom Mund
in die Hand.

May trouble thrive. As long as you have it
you're still alive.

Burn a bright torch and understand
so you can make it
from mouth
to hand.

Kondolationen

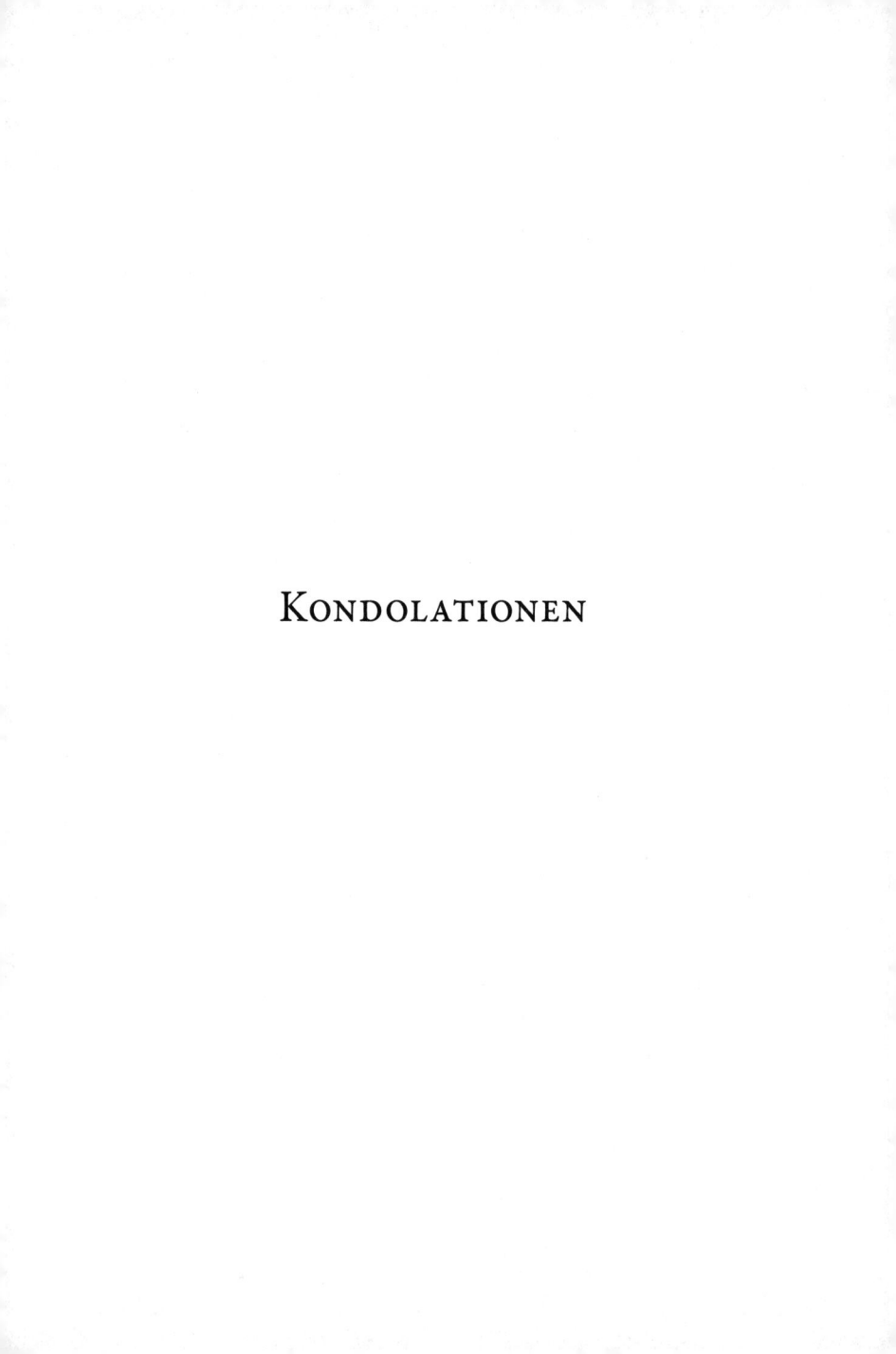

Condolences

Bericht über Horst K.
oder Die Besserung des Menschen

1

Aufgewachsen ohne Mutter,
der Vater ein Trinker.
Mit vierzehn, mit sechzehn,
dann Einweisung ins Heim.
Mit zwanzig ein drittes Mal.
Fünfzehn Jahre insgesamt,
kleine Delikte: das Eigentum anderer.
Nicht etwa Picasso
oder ein Gang durch die Bank.
Fahrrad, Aktentasche,
ein schlecht sitzender Mantel
doch warm.
Rückfälle: Zechprellerei.

Nun aber Schluß, lieber Freund,
nun aber geht's aufwärts,
sanft und guten Willens
in ein fröhliches Leben.
Herzlichen Glückwunsch,
der Platz an der Sonne
ist frei.

Report on Horst K.,
or The Rehabilitation of the Individual

1

Raised without a mother,
the father a drinker.
Once at fourteen, again at sixteen
then off to a facility.
At twenty a third time.
Fifteen years in total,
petty crimes: the possessions of others.
Not a Picasso
or a run through the bank.
Bicycle, brief case,
a coat, ill-fitting
but warm.
Backsliding: slipping out on the check.

Enough of that, my friend,
now things are looking up,
with gentleness and hope
into a happy life.
Congratulations,
a spot on the sunny side
has opened up.

2

Einbruch in ein leerstehendes Haus,
Verzehr von Konserven, Benutzung eines Betts.
Das war kürzlich.
Der Winter ist hart.
Und schon wieder
sitzt er im Warmen.
Sie erinnern sich.
Es war in der Zeitung zu lesen.
Wir sind überfordert
und härten uns ab.

3

Nach der Entlassung
nun endlich der bessere Mensch.
In der letzten Nacht des Jahres
nahm er Zuflucht,
legte sich in den Wald und erfror.
Es war in der Zeitung zu lesen.
Der Engel, mit dem er den Wald verließ
bleibt unerwähnt.

2

Forced entry into an empty house,
consumption of canned food, use of a bed.
That wasn't long ago.
The winter is hard.
Then once again
doing time in the warmth.
They remember it.
A story appeared in the paper.
It's too much to bear
and we become hardened.

3

After release
a rehabilitated man at last.
In the final night of the year
he took refuge,
laid himself down in the woods and froze.
A story appeared in the paper.
The angel who carried him out of the woods
is not mentioned.

Der Hirtenknabe von Lenbach

1

Mein Bild, das nie mir gehörte,
hing im Studierzimmer meines Onkels
unweit des leicht angehobenen Kopfteils
einer Liege zu Ruhezwecken,
so daß sich der Ruhende
ein Bild machen mußte.

Während der Onkel studierte,
betrachtete ich liegend
die schmutzigen Füße des Knaben
auch die unordentliche Kleidung
mit Befremden
und mein reinliches Kleid.
Ich prüfte die unbewegliche Hand
über den Augen.
Darüber wurde es blau
und ich fürchtete mich.

2

Nach Jahrzehnten sehe ich ihn wieder.
Das war gestern, unerwartet,
das blieb von einem alten Pfarrhaus,
überm Kirschbaumsekretär.

The Shepherd Boy by Lenbach

1

My picture, though one I never owned,
hung in my uncle's study
facing the recliner
with the back tilted up a bit,
so the picture was impressed
upon the mind of the one reclining.

While my uncle studied,
I leaned back and thought about
the boy's dirty feet
and his disheveled clothes
with unease
then my clean dress.
I stared at the stiff hand
covering his eyes.
Up above the sky went blue
and I was afraid.

2

Decades later I meet him again.
That was yesterday, unexpected,
the picture over the cherry desk
of an old parsonage.

Der Knabe heil ganz ohne Riß.
Der Knabe der da hat gesiegt.
Der Knabe überlebt.
Und über ihm und immer noch
der antwortlos vom Blau
verstellte Himmel.

The boy safe and sound.
The boy, he won out.
The boy survives.
And above him still, hidden
by so much blue, the sky
gives no answer.

Der Augenblick

Der Augenblick
verweilt
wie lang
das Schwarz wird Licht
die neue Jahreszeit
die Jahre gehn
siehst du denn nicht
sie sterben
alle.

Der Augenblick
ist schon vorüber,
ein Menschenalter
goldne Zeit.
Ich übe Disziplin
und leugne jeden Schmerz.
Du weißt, wovon ich rede.

The Moment

The moment
lingers
how long
blackness becomes light
the new season
the years go by
don't you see
they die
one and all.

The moment
is already over,
a lifetime
golden age.
I am disciplined
and deny every pain.
You know what I'm talking about.

Grablied

Rosen rot und Veilchen
ein Weilchen
du weißt ja
bist du schon tot
daß die Bäume
zu Häupten, zu Füßen
alt werden wie Wald.
Vom schönen Fleisch
ist geblieben was blinkt.
Knochen allüberall.

An diesem Tag im Frühling
Sommer Herbst und Winter.

Funeral Song

Violets and roses red
 a little while
and—you know—
you're already dead
and the trees
at the head, at the foot
grow old as forest.
Of lovely flesh
just flashes remain.
Bones everywhere and all around.

On this day in spring
summer fall and winter.

Der Tod eines Mädchens

Infarkt, Thrombose, Embolie
welche Worte
für ein Mädchen schmal
wie ein Kind und wie neu.

Ruh dich aus
oder willst du hinaus?
Es will Abend werden und Frühling.
Die Stadt ist weit und eng.
In den Kolonnaden hängen
die bläulichen Wolken
betriebsamer Autos.
Das sticht in die Schläfen
ein wenig und fein.
Der Scirocco ergreift dir
das Herz.
Kommst du hinaus
oder bist du zu müd
und willst sterben.
Dann bleib ich, bleib ich
bei dir.

Death of a Girl

Infarction, thrombosis, embolism
such words
for a girl small
as a child and so new.

Rest up now
or do you want out?
Evening wants to come on, and spring.
The city is vast and closed in.
Bluish clouds
from scurrying cars
hang in the colonnades.
This throbs in your temples,
slight and sweet.
The Scirocco wind takes hold of
your heart.
Will you come out
or are you too tired
and ready for death?
Then I'll stay, I'll stay
with you.

Stillstand

Ich stehe still und horche,
ob ich weitergehe und
weitergehend finde, was
sich wünschen ließe.
Und sei's ein Wort.
Zum Beispiel eines,
das den Zauber riefe
als wär's verbrieft. Als sei
aus Gold auf Stein ein Grab
verschrieben, das Beide
nun verriete. Wo Beide
tun, als ob sie schliefen,
die doch vor langer Zeit
den Ort verließen, der
möchte, daß sie sich
entschließen,
still zu stehn.

Standstill

I stand still and listen,
should I move on and
in moving on see what
can still be dreamed.
And if only of a word
then one
that conjures alchemy
as if guaranteed. As if set
in stone in gold on a grave
for all to read, so both
can be perceived. Where both
pretend they're sound asleep,
though from this place
they've taken leave, this
place that wants them
to agree
to stand still.

Um Mitternacht

Hat alles begonnen.
War fein ersonnen.

Ist vorübergegangen.
Hat neu angefangen.
Ist wieder vergangen.

Und immer so fort.
So steht es geschrieben.
Nichts ist geblieben.

Zur zwölften Stunde
tritt die Kunde
hervor, schreitet durchs Tor
und hinüber.
Die Augen gehen dir über.

Ein Grund zu erbleichen.
Zum Steinerweichen.
Bleich wie der Mond.

At Midnight

When things began
a beautiful plan.

Once already past
restarted up fast.
But it didn't last.

Then over and over.
It was ordained
nothing remained.

At the twelfth stroke
the truth is evoked
and certain, strides through the curtain
and disappears.
Your eyes fill with tears.

A reason to pale.
A fate to bewail.
Pale as the moon.

Von anderen bedenklichen Anlässen

Of Other
Questionable Occasions

MÖGLICHKEITEN

Ein kleiner Wink nur
und schon fällt vom Hals
ohne die Spur eines Zögerns
der Kopf.

Oder er steigt
der Mensch mit dem Kopf
höher, sehr hoch
im Flug.

Oder er sinkt ins Verlies
verlassen vom Geist,
verwaist.

So ist es wahr,
uns wird ein Haar
gekrümmt werden auf Erden.

Possibilities

Just a little nod,
and without a second thought
your head can fall
right off your shoulders.

Or it can rise,
you with your head,
higher, very high
in flight.

Or sink into the dungeon
abandoned by spirit,
orphaned.

As it is said,
a hair on your head
will be harmed here on earth.

REDEN WIR NICHT MEHR von Landschaft.
Reden wir vom fein kalkulierten Netz
der Längen- und Breitengrade
von den bläulichen Ozeanen
und den hellen Flecken der Kontinente.
Reden wir von den berührbaren Polen
einer sanft rotierenden Kugel
von der gefahrlosen Dürre der Wüsten
dem verläßlichen Grün der Wildnisse
dem Geraschel von Tier und Mensch
und von den punktgenauen Städten.
Betreten wir demnächst und entledigt
die Milchstraße. Der Ausweg
für die unbelehrbaren Metaphern.

LET'S NOT TALK about landscape anymore.
Let's talk about the fine mathematical net
of longitude and latitude
about the blue-tinged oceans
and the bright patches of the continents.
Let's talk about the exposed poles
of this gently spinning globe
about the contained drought of the desert,
the reliable green of the wilderness,
the rustle of animal and human
and about the perfectly formed cities.
Let's head off soon for the Milky Way,
relieved of this burden. The way out
for metaphors who never learn.

Traum

Der Berg zerbricht.
Das Licht ersticht
die Erhabenen.
Und die weniger Erhabenen
fallen ins Knie
wie nie zuvor.

Vorüber der Plunder von Jahr und Tag,
die sieben Freuden, die Plagen.
Hab ich geträumt.

Dream

The mountain crumbles.
Light strikes down
the sublime.
And the less lofty
fall to their knees
like never before.

Gone the flotsam of year and day,
gone the seven blessings, the plagues.
This I dreamed.

Verweigerung der Aussage

Später, viel später
wenn der Täter alt geworden ist
und das Opfer vergeßlich
wie ein Sieb

werde ich mich
zu erinnern suchen
und fluchen weil
das Gedächtnis nichts hält.

Später, viel später
werde ich zu Protokoll geben
was ich nicht weiß.

Refusal to Testify

Later, much later
when the perpetrator has grown old
and the victim forgetful
as a sieve

I will
try to remember
and curse because
my memory retains nothing.

Later, much later
I will bear witness to
what I don't know.

Utopie

Es freut mich die Übermacht der Vokale.
Schreckensrufe könnten es sein.
Oder im trüben Gewässer ein glasklarer Schein,
der blinkt und sinkt.
So tief kann ein Grund doch nicht sein,
daß wir ihn nicht fänden
gebunden an Füßen und Händen.

Utopia

The domination of the vowels makes me happy.
Perhaps the sounds are screams of fright.
Or in murky waters the appearance of light
blinking and sinking.
A reason cannot be so deep
that it cannot be found
even with hands and feet bound.

Erinnerung

Von all den Heerscharen
ist uns der Eine geblieben.
Mit seinem Schwert
von siebenfacher Perfektion
wird er uns jagen.
Noch einmal schöpfen wir Atem
wie in Kindertagen.

Memory

Of all the armies,
we are left with just this one.
With a sword
of sevenfold perfection
it will hunt us.
We stop to catch our breath again
like we did as children.

Protokoll

Am Abend des 25. gegen 23 Uhr
sehe ich an der Küchenwand
zwischen Delfter und Thymian
grundlos stehe ich da
um das Licht zu löschen
eine gerahmte Fotografie.

Sie zeigt zwei Kinder
seit dreißig Jahren
mit gehorsam gescheiteltem Haar
geordnetem Kragen
und einem Lächeln
in Erwartung des Augenblicks
an dem ich es wahrnehmen werde.

Statement

On the evening of the 25th toward 11 pm,
I'm standing in the kitchen for no good reason
just to turn off the light
when I see there on the wall
between old blue crockery and thyme
a framed photograph.

For thirty years
a picture of two children
hair parted neatly
collars nice and straight
and smiles
in anticipation of the moment
that I will finally notice.

Falsches Lied

In einem stillen Grunde,
da ging ein Mühlenrad.
Der Müller ist verschwunden,
der dort gemahlen hat.

Da wollt der Bach nicht fließen,
der Wind wollt nicht mehr gehn,
das Korn wollt nicht mehr sprießen.
So blieb das Mühlrad stehn.

Im Hause ist es dunkel,
doch niemand mehr macht Licht.
Nur noch die Mäuse suchen
nach Korn und finden's nicht.

A Different Song

Within a quiet valley
a mill turned night and day
and there the miller was
before he went away.

And so the stream refused to flow,
the grain refused to sprout,
the wind decided not to blow,
the mill had been phased out.

The dark of night has fallen,
no people making light.
The mice alone still search
for grain and find nothing tonight.

AN EIN KIND

Wenn wir lange genug warten,
dann wird es kommen.
Heute noch, fragt das Kind.
Heut oder morgen. Ein Schiff,
mußt du wissen, braucht Zeit.
So weit und breit wie das Meer.
Dann bist du groß.
Dann steigen wir ein
und machen die Reise.
Zusammen. Wir beide.
Und jeder auf seine Weise.

To a Child

If we wait long enough,
it will come.
Sometime today, the child asks.
Today or tomorrow. You know
how ships can take their time.
The ocean is so far and wide.
Then you'll be big.
Then we'll climb aboard
and make the trip.
Together. The two of us.
And each in our own way.

Vom Öffnen des Fensters

On Opening the Window

MORGENS

1

Frühmorgens sehe ich
ich wollte vorübergehen
im Fenster die Kastanie voll Licht.
Dies ist der Frühling,
denke ich,
und gehe zur Arbeit.
Sie ist freundlich
und erlaubt mir
Gedichte über den Frühling zu lesen.

2

Ich öffne das Fenster
im nächtlichen Morgen
und sehe
auf das Licht der Sterne
antworten Laternen.
In Reihen die Autos
wie schlafende Tiere.
Und gegenüber
wo die Männer ein- und ausgehn,
brennt bei den Frauen
Licht.

In the Morning

1

Early in the morning I see,
just in passing,
the chestnut full of light in the window.
This is spring,
I think,
and go to work,
which is friendly
and allows me
to read poems about springtime.

2

I open the window
in the dark of the morning
and see
how the streetlights answer
the light of the stars.
Rows of cars
like animals sleeping.
And across the way
where the men come and go,
by the women, burning
light.

Liebes Land

Denk
Einmal nach, sagte ich mir.
Und ich denke:
Tag und Nacht bist du nur halb
So viel wert, sieh das
Chaos deiner Kehrseiten
Hektisch, gründlich und
Leitfähig bist du.
Angst wurde dir
Nie, auch nicht vor
Dir selbst.

Dear Country

Stop
And think, I told myself.
And I think:
By day by night, you're worth only
Half as much, look at the
Chaos of your flip sides
Frenzied, thorough and
Conductive—that's you.
You've never been afraid,
Not even of
Yourself.

Billionenfache Vergrösserung

Der Hut meiner Mutter
ist nur ein kleiner Hut,
in einem Blau, das die Farbe Lila
 eben erfindet, aus feinstem Stroh,
den Flechtkünsten der Jahrhunderte.

Der von der Berührung des Sommers lebt,
der Hut meiner Mutter,
ist nicht mehr auffindbar.

Der Verlust nimmt Ausmaße an
daß sich die Zeiten verfinstern.
Nicht inbegriffen
der Rest dieser Welt.

Magnified by a Trillion

My mother's hat
is only a small hat
in a blue that promises
the color purple, of the finest straw
centuries of craft in the plaiting.

Alive through the touch of summer,
my mother's hat
is now long gone.

The loss takes on such proportions
that the times grow dark.
For all but
the rest of this world.

PAUSENZEICHEN

Wie beruhigend
wieder und wieder
neue Beweise zu erhalten
von der Unerschöpflichkeit
der Beweisenden:
so daß du entbunden bist
von den Tugenden derjenigen
die den Frieden erhalten
wie ein verendendes Masttier.
Die Beispiele bieten sich an.
Wir nennen sie alle beim Namen,
wie die Wolken da oben, umflutet vom Blau
über den grünlichen Höhen
der Vogesen bis es Nacht wird.
Ja, Nacht.

Signature Tune

How soothing
to receive new proof
over and over
from the inexhaustibility
of the provers:
so that you are released
from the virtues of those
who keep the peace,
like livestock wasting away.
Examples are everywhere.
We call them all by name,
like the clouds over the green peaks
of the Vosges surrounded by blue
until night falls.
Yes, night.

BERICHT VOM ENDE DER BELAGERUNG EINER PERSON

Im Augenblick äußerster Not
greife ich zu den Waffen.

Ich bedrohe die mich Bedrohenden
Ich lasse im Stich die mich im Stich Lassenden
Ich kündige den Notdürftigen
Ich trenne das Wort ab von den Rednern
Ich hinterlasse die Halbheiten
und die Mitleidenschaften
Ich setze mich ab von der Berechenbarkeit der Tage
und der Unberechenbarkeit.
Ich bereite dem Ende ein Ende.

Ich beginne den Anfang vom Anfang
Ich ordne die Giebel des Dachs
und ich ordne die Zeiger der Uhr
und verwildere die Zweige des Herzens
und stehe auf.
Auf Befehl des allerhöchsten Ich.

Report on the Liberation of a Person Under Siege

In the moment of extreme emergency
I go for the weapons.

I threaten those who threaten me
I abandon those who abandon me
I fire the makeshift
I separate the speaker from his word
I leave behind half-measures
and unintended consequences
I distance myself from the predictability of the day
and from unpredictability.
I put an end to the end.

I start the beginning from the beginning
I arrange the gables of the roof
and I arrange the hands on the clock
and I let the branches of my heart grow wild
and I stand up.
Under orders of my highest self.

Wer lebt

Who Lives

Alter jüdischer Friedhof im Mai

Wer lebt hier
Ich höre vereinzelt Gesang
und den Sprung des Eichhorns hinab.

Wer ist hier der Herr
Aufrecht horchen die Steine.

Wer wirft das Kleid
Es fällt der Schatten von Bäumen
Es fällt das Licht aus der Hand.

Wer geht durch das Gras
Sieh doch. Die Stille.

Old Jewish Cemetery in May

Who lives here
I hear scattered singing
and a squirrel jumping down.

Who is the master here
The stones stand and listen.

Who casts the dress
Shadows drop from trees
Light drops from the hand.

Who moves through the grass
Just look. The silence.

Der Olivenbaum im Garten Gethsemane

Vor zweitausend Jahren schon,
heißt es, hat er gesehn,
war er, was war denn,
so sag doch, wach auf.

Dunkler Winkel deines Gartens
Festung deines Herrn
Vorhof seiner Gegenwart

Nach zweitausend Jahren noch
ein grünes Blatt das wacht.
Ein Schein ein Licht ein Leuchten
ein Morgen- und ein Abendmal.

The Olive Tree in the Garden of Gethsemane

Over two thousand years ago,
they say, it saw,
it was, what was it,
come tell me, wake up.

Dark corner of your garden
Fortress of your Lord
Forecourt to his presence

Still two thousand years later
a green leaf that keeps watch.
A shine, a light, a glow
the day's first meal, the last supper.

Alte Uhr

Es öffnet sich der Kreis
und schließt.
Ein Spiel mit Zeigern
eins bis zwölf
nicht eine fehlt.
Wo ist die Stunde der Metapher.

Wie Samt glänzt das Gehäuse.
Wie Samt der Weg
der ganz nach innen führt.
Dem Herzschlag treu
steht sie dort unerreichbar
still.

Old Clock

The circle opens
and closes.
A play of hands,
one through twelve
not one missing.
Where is the hour of the metaphor.

Like velvet the outside shines.
Like velvet the path
that leads all the way in
where it stands true
to the heartbeat, unreachably
still.

Einfache Dinge

Einerlei geh ich
Zweierlei seh ich
Dreierlei leb ich
Viererlei freut mich am Tage

Einerlei sag ich nicht
Zweierlei trag ich nicht
Dreierlei hab ich nicht
Viererlei schreckt mich zu Tode

Simple Things

I go when it's all the same
In twos I see
In threes I live
And four things bring joy to my day

I don't speak when it's all the same
In twos I don't carry
In threes I don't have
And four things scare me to death

BESTÄNDIGE DINGE

Des Goldschmieds Gold, das nicht verkommt
Des Malers Bild aus Kunst gemacht
Die Logik des Lichts am Ende des Tunnels.

Die Mauern sind hart ehe sie fallen
Das Haus steht fest ehe es stürzt

Was soll ich mehr sagen
Die Zeit ist kurz.

Reliable Things

The goldsmith's gold that never breaks down
The painter's picture made of art
The logic of the light at the end of the tunnel.

The walls are solid before they crumble
The house stands strong before it falls

What else is there to say
Time is short.

ERINNERUNG AN ARP

Ach, aber ach, sagt Paul Klee
schließt ein Auge
und grämt sich.
Denkt er an *Lieschen*
als es noch klein war,
an *Traumhaftes*,
an den *zukünftigen Feind*.

Ach, sage ich, wer kann
es denn wissen. Ich denke
an Arp und den Bahnsteig
zu Frankfurt. Es schlagen
die Türen und Fenster.

Ach, aber ach. Ins Sichtbare
weißt du
kommt keiner zurück.

Memory of Arp

Ach and ach again, Paul Klee says,
closing an eye,
and grieves.
Does he think about *Lieschen*
when she was still small,
about the *stuff of dreams*,
about the *future enemy*.

Ach, I say, who can
ever know. I think
about Arp and the platform
in Frankfurt. The doors
and windows slam.

Ach and ach again. No one,
you know,
returns to the world of the visible.

Ordnung

So hoch die Nacht überm Tag
So fern der Abend vom Morgen
Licht, Blume, Busch, Baum etc.
Das ist der Geheimbund
Das ist die Ordnung

Order

As high as the night above the day
As far as the evening from the morning
Light, flower, bush, tree, etc.
This is the secret pact
This is the order of things

DAS LICHT gib uns heute
und vergib uns die Müdigkeit
wenn der Herbst leuchtet
und die Taubheit
wenn uns das Hören vergeht
und die Blindheit
wenn uns ein Sehender streift
und die Lähmung
wenn wir begabt sind zu gehen
und die Trübung
wenn es an Fröhlichkeit nicht mangelt
und die Leere
wenn wir nicht wissen wer wir sind
und die Verzagtheit
wenn wir den Mut nicht achten.
Wenn die Stimme schwach wird
wer hört dann aufs Wort.

GIVE US THIS DAY the light
and forgive us our listlessness
when the autumn glows
and deafness
when our hearing takes leave
and blindness
when we're finally seen
and paralysis
when we know it's time to go
and gloominess
when there's no lack of cheer
and emptiness
when we don't know ourselves
and despair
when we ignore courage.
When the voice grows faint—
who can hear the word.

Wanderungen

Wir, unser schwerstes Gepäck,
verlassen die Zone des Regens
und gehen hinauf auf den Berg der Sonne.
Er ist sehr herrlich.

Und wir, unser schwerstes Gepäck,
verlassen den Berg der Sonne
und kehren zurück in die Zone des Regens.
Das ist beschwerlich.

Journeys

We, our own heaviest load,
leave the zone of rain
and hike up the mountain of the sun.
It's fantastic.

And we, our own heaviest load,
leave the mountain of the sun
and head back to the zone of rain.
That is tragic.

Herbst

Wie die Kirchtürme zittern im Licht
wir werden es nicht überleben.
Wie wir uns täuschen lassen
vom Licht, das die Türme bewegt.

Autumn

The way the church towers tremble in the light
we will not survive this.
The way we let ourselves be fooled
by the light that sets the towers moving.

Die 7 Stationen eines langen künstlich beleuchteten Gangs

Vom Bewußtsein schwindender Natürlichkeit
Vom eiszeitlichen Gefälle eines Lufthauchs
Vom Schmerz, der den Knochen erhellt
Vom Schlagen kahlgefrorener Flügel
Vom heimlichen Entgleisen eines Augenpaars
Vom dunklen höchstrichterlichen Stuhl
Noch hör' ich die Glocke nicht läuten.

The 7 Stations of a Long Artificially Lit Passage

By the awareness of nature's fading glow
By the glacial decline of a breath
By the pain that illuminates the bones
By the beat of frost-barren wings
By the secret stillness in a pair of eyes
By the dark seat of highest judgment
I can almost hear the bell ring.

Trauerbänder

Als sie gegangen war
es war nach der achten Stunde
unter den Schnee

ist geblieben die Welt
wie sie ist.

Die Kränze haben sich
lange gehalten in der Kälte
die nicht gehen will
wenn Frühling wird.

Wir kehren immer aufs neue zurück
wer aber käme noch heim.

Black Bands of Mourning

When she went
under the snow,
it was after the eighth hour,

the world remained
as it is.

The wreaths lasted
a long time in the cold
which never wants to leave
when spring approaches.

We return here again and again
but does anybody ever come home.

Ich betrete nicht den Festsaal der Sätze
die Gemächer der vor Grazie sich biegenden Nebensätze
die würdigen Hügel des Partizips.
Ich überlasse mich nicht den geschmeidigen Perioden
dem rauschhaften Absturz
den komödiantischen Untiefen.
Ich verweigere den Müßiggang der Addition
das Manöver der Unklarheit
die Dämmerung der Klarheit.
Ich stimme nicht an das Lied zur Verführung der minderjährigen Ewigkeit.
Ich lehne ab das Plagiat der Klage des Windes und des Flächenbrandes.
Ich bediene mich der Notdürftigkeit:
Sie ist gestorben
verdorben
und verfalle der irdischen Einfalt
dem Trost des himmlischen Fests.

I will not enter the ballroom of sentences
the chamber of clauses that bow to grace,
the worthy heights of the participle.
I will not give myself over to supple punctuation,
to the intoxicating fall,
to the theatrical shallows.
I reject the idleness of addition
the maneuvers of uncertainty
the twilight of certainty.
I will not sing an ode to the seduction of premature eternity.
I refuse the plagiarism of moaning wind and wildfire.
I reach for the essential,
she has died
decayed,
and I turn to earthly innocence,
to the consolation of the heavenly feast.

Kein Wort fällt tief
und keines das den Lerchen gleicht
Kein Leuchten
Keine Langsamkeit
Kein Atem
Kein Wohin
Die Nacht kein Jubel und
ein Trauerband dem Tag

No WORD falls far
and none are like the larks
No light
No slowness
No breath
No elsewhere
In the night, no cries of joy and
a black band of mourning for the day

KALEIDOSKOP

Sonne Mond und Stern.
Zeig her. Die Brocken
machen Weltgeschichte.
Laß sehn, was unsre
Horizonte täglich
übersteigt.

Schön dreht sich mir
das Rad. Das Auge glüht.
Wie sich's verzweigt.
Gib her die Mitte
dieser Pracht.
Wir haben alles
zu verlieren.
Den Tag, die Nacht.

Kaleidoscope

Sun moon and star.
Let me see. These giants
make the world turn
round. Show me what
rises above our horizons
every day.

Beautiful wheel turning
for me. Eye aglow.
The way it branches out.
Give me the center
of this glory.
We have everything
to lose.
The day, the night.

Was alles braucht's zum Paradies

Ein Warten ein Garten
eine Mauer darum
ein Tor mit viel Schloß und Riegel
ein Schwert eine Schneide aus Morgenlicht
ein Rauschen aus Blättern und Bächen
ein Flöten ein Harfen ein Zirpen
ein Schnauben (von lieblicher Art)
Arzneien aus Balsam und Düften
viel Immergrün und Nimmerschwarz
kein Plagen Klagen Hoffen
kein Ja kein Nein kein Widerspruch
ein Freudenlaut
ein allerlei Wiegen und Wogen
das Spielzeug eine Acht aus Gold
ein Heute und kein Morgen
der Zeitvertreib das Wunder
das Testament aus warmem Schnee
wer kommt wer ginge wieder
Wir werden es erfragen.

All You Need for Paradise

A guard a yard
and a wall all around
a gate with latch and lock
a sword a blade of the morning's light
the whoosh of leaf and stream
a trill a pluck a chirp
a snort (of the cheerful kind)
medicine of balm and aroma
lots of evergreen and nevergray
no moaning groaning hoping
neither yes or no, nor contradiction
a joyful sound
all sorts of tossing and turning
toys and games, a golden eight
a today and no tomorrow
the pass-time the miracle
the testament of warm snow
who'll come, who'll go again
We will find out.

Acknowledgments

I am grateful to so many people for long and wonderful conversations about these poems, in particular to my German friends Silvana Nitsch and Alena Moser; and to Lauren Paredes, Andrew Chenevert, Michael Shay and so many other members of the Eastside Poetry Workshop. Everything you all do inspires me!

Thank you, Rachel Mulder, for enthusiastically sharing your beautiful typewriter art for the cover of this book!

I would also like to gratefully acknowledge The Broadsided Press and Janice Redman for creating such a beautiful broadside of "The Silent One." Julia Maas and others at the Deutsche Literaturarchiv Marbach graciously helped me research Elisabeth Borchers and took extra steps to get the material I was looking for. Thank you!

Finally, thank you, Carl and Natalie. There's no way around it—you two are the best!

—Caroline Wilcox Reul

Biographies

ELISABETH BORCHERS was born in 1926 and raised bilingually with French and German. She worked as an editor, first at Luchterhand, then at Suhrkamp from 1960 until her retirement in 1998. She is often cited as playing a critical role in the development of German literature during the second half of the 20th century. She is the author of eight books of poetry, numerous children's books, radio plays and essays and has translated many books from French into German. She died in 2013 in Frankfurt.

CAROLINE WILCOX REUL lived in Germany for ten years, working as an English teacher and freelance lexicographer. She has a MA in computational linguistics and German language and literature from the Ludwig-Maximilians-Universität in Munich.

Tavern Books

Tavern Books is a not-for-profit poetry publisher that exists to print, promote, and preserve works of literary vision, to foster a climate of cultural preservation, and to disseminate books in a way that benefits the reading public.

We publish books in translation from the world's finest poets, champion new works by innovative writers, and revive out-of-print classics. We keep our titles in print, honoring the cultural contract between publisher and author, as well as between publisher and public. Our catalog, known as The Living Library, sustains the visions of our authors, ensuring their voices remain alive in the social and artistic discourse of our modern era.

Subscriptions

Become a subscriber and receive the next six Tavern Books titles at a substantial discount, delivered to your door. Paperback and hardcover subscriptions available.

For details visit www.tavernbooks.org/subscriptions or write to us at:

Tavern Books
at Union Station
800 NW 6th Avenue #255
Portland, Oregon 97209

The Living Library

Killing Floor by Ai

Arthur's Talk with the Eagle by Anonymous,
translated from the Welsh by Gwyneth Lewis

Ashulia by Zubair Ahmed

Breckinridge County Suite by Joe Bolton

My People & Other Poems by Wojciech Bonowicz,
translated from the Polish by Piotr Florczyk

Who Lives by Elisabeth Borchers,
translated from the German by Caroline Wilcox Reul

Buson: Haiku by Yosa Buson,
translated from the Japanese by Franz Wright

Poems 1904 by C.P. Cavafy,
translated from the Greek by Paul Merchant

Evidence of What Is Said by Ann Charters and Charles Olson

Who Whispered Near Me by Killarney Clary

The End of Space by Albert Goldbarth

Six-Minute Poems: The Last Poems
by George Hitchcock

The Wounded Alphabet: Collected Poems
by George Hitchcock

Hitchcock on Trial
by George Hitchcock

At the Devil's Banquets by Anise Koltz,
translated from the French by John F. Deane

My Blue Piano by Else Lasker-Schüler,
translated from the German by Eavan Boland

Why We Live in the Dark Ages by Megan Levad

Archeology by Adrian C. Louis

Fire Water World & Among the Dog Eaters
by Adrian C. Louis

Emergency Brake by Ruth Madievsky

Under an Arkansas Sky by Jo McDougall

The Undiscovered Room by Jo McDougall

Ocean by Joseph Millar

Petra by Amjad Nasser,
translated from the Arabic by Fady Joudah

The Fire's Journey: Part I by Eunice Odio,
translated from the Spanish by Keith Ekiss
with Sonia P. Ticas and Mauricio Espinoza

The Fire's Journey: Part II by Eunice Odio,
translated from the Spanish by Keith Ekiss
with Sonia P. Ticas and Mauricio Espinoza

*The Fire's Journey: Part III by Eunice Odio,
translated from the Spanish by Keith Ekiss
with Sonia P. Ticas and Mauricio Espinoza

*The Fire's Journey: Part IV by Eunice Odio,
translated from the Spanish by Keith Ekiss
with Sonia P. Ticas and Mauricio Espinoza

Full Body Pleasure Suit by Elsbeth Pancrazi

Duino Elegies by Rainer Maria Rilke,
translated from the German by Gary Miranda

Twelve Poems About Cavafy by Yannis Ritsos,
translated from the Greek by Paul Merchant

*Monochords by Yannis Ritsos,
translated from the Greek by Paul Merchant

Glowing Enigmas by Nelly Sachs,
translated from the German by Michael Hamburger

Prodigy by Charles Simic,
drawings by Charles Seluzicki

Night of Shooting Stars by Leonardo Sinisgalli,
translated from the Italian by W. S. Di Piero

Skin by Tone Škrjanec,
translated from the Slovene by Matthew Rohrer and Ana Pepelnik

We Women by Edith Södergran,
translated from the Swedish by Samuel Charters

Winterward by William Stafford

Building the Barricade by Anna Świrszczyńska,
translated from the Polish by Piotr Florczyk

Baltics by Tomas Tranströmer,
with photographs by Ann Charters,
translated from the Swedish by Samuel Charters

For the Living and the Dead by Tomas Tranströmer,
translated from the Swedish by John F. Deane

*forthcoming

Tavern Books is funded, in part, by the generosity of philanthropic organizations, public and private institutions, and individual donors. By supporting Tavern Books and its mission, you enable us to publish the most exciting poets from around the world. To learn more about underwriting Tavern Books titles, please contact us by e-mail: info@tavernbooks.org.

MAJOR FUNDING HAS BEEN PROVIDED BY

Lannan THE LIBRA FOUNDATION

OREGON ARTS COMMISSION

ART WORKS.

National Endowment for the Arts
arts.gov

GOETHE INSTITUT

THE PUBLICATION OF THIS BOOK IS MADE POSSIBLE, IN PART, BY THE SUPPORT OF THE FOLLOWING INDIVIDUALS

Sophie Cabot Black
Audrey Block
Joe Bratcher
Dean & Karen Garyet
Daniel Handler
Kate Harbour
Ana Jokkmokk
Jennifer Jones & Mark Swartz
Leah Middlebrook
Joseph Millar & Dorianne Laux

Jay Ponteri
Mary Ann Ryan
Donna Swartz
Mary Szybist & Jerry Harp
Bill & Leah Stenson
Jonathan Wells
Dan Wieden
Wendy Willis & David Biespiel
Vince & Patty Wixon
Ron & Kathy Wrolstad

Colophon

This book was designed and typeset by Eldon Potter at Bryan Potter Design, Portland, Oregon. Text is set in Garamond, an old-style serif typeface named for the punch-cutter Claude Garamond (c. 1480-1561). *Who Lives* appears in both paperback and cloth-covered editions. Printed on archival-quality paper by McNaughton & Gunn, Inc.